BE THE CHANGE!

CLIMATE EMERGENCY

HOW YOU CAN MAKE A DIFFERENCE

Cynthia O'Brien

BROWN BEAR BOOK

T0286239

Published by Brown Bear Books Ltd

4877 N. Circulo Bujia
Tucson, AZ 85718
USA

and

G14, Regent Studios
1 Thane Villas
London N7 7PH
UK

ISBN 978-1-78121-944-7 (ALB)
ISBN 978-1-78121-950-8 (paperback)

Library of Congress Cataloging-in-Publication Data available on request

Design Manager: Keith Davis
Children's Publisher: Anne O'Daly
Picture Manager: Sophie Mortimer

Picture Credits
Cover: Shutterstock: Holli (background), New Africa; Interior: Alamy: Belga News Agency 12, Michael
Wheatley 23, Xinhua 11; iStock: SolStock 26, South Agency 16, Jarno Verdonk 22, A.J. Watt 25; Shutterstock:
Stef Bennett 21, Jacek Chabraszewski 15, Ringo Chiu 20, Sheila Fitzgerald 29, Daniel Freyr 6, Nady Ginzburg 8,
Halfpoint 27, Kathy Hutchins 12, Maria Igisheva 14, PARALAXIS 9, Phil Pasquini 10, Prostock-studio 24, Mamunur
Rashid 5, Rejdan 4, stocksre 18, Uplight Pictures 17, Rolf G Wackenberg 19, Lee Wooseung 7

All artwork and other photography Brown Bear Books.

Brown Bear Books has made every attempt to contact the copyright holder.
If you have any information about omissions, please contact: licensing@brownbearbooks.co.uk

Manufactured in the United States of America
CPSIA compliance information: Batch#AG/5657

Websites
The website addresses in this book were valid at the time of going to press. However, it is possible
that contents or addresses may change following publication of this book. No responsibility for
any such changes can be accepted by the author or the publisher. Readers should be supervised
when they access the Internet.

Contents

Introduction

Earth is in trouble. Climate change and a rapidly warming planet are resulting in rising sea levels, habitat loss, drought, flooding, and many other issues. Record-breaking heatwaves are becoming more common. Fighting climate change has become an urgent priority.

Throughout Earth's 4.5-billion-year history, there is evidence of climate change, from long ice ages to warmer periods. The difference today is the rate at which global warming is happening. It is part of an overall climate change that is having disastrous effects on the planet.

The Issues

The impacts of climate change are wide-ranging. Extreme heat threatens all life on Earth. Destructive wildfires wipe out forests and animal habitats as well as homes and other human-made structures. Droughts make it difficult or impossible to grow crops and leave people without enough drinking water. Severe storms, such as hurricanes, bring widespread flooding.

Droughts are a serious environmental threat, affecting crops, people, and animals. Climate change is making them happen more frequently.

Activists in Bangladesh take part in the Global Climate Strike. In this annual protest, young people around the world take to the streets, calling for government action on the climate crisis.

A Global Fight

Millions of young people around the world are already making a difference in the fight against climate change. Youth-led organizations, such as Earth Uprising, Fridays for Future, and This is Zero Hour, empower young people to challenge leaders, spread awareness, and be involved in decision making. In March 2023, the United Nations appointed seven young climate activists to its second Youth Advisory Group on Climate Change.

Chapter 1

Understanding the Arguments

In the 1800s, some scientists realized that certain gases in the atmosphere could overheat the planet. Many others were skeptical until studies in the 1950s and 1960s began to confirm that Earth was heating up. By the 1980s, scientific evidence proved that climate change and global warming were real, and that action needed to be taken.

To understand climate change over Earth's history, scientists look at natural records, such as ancient rocks, coral reefs, and tree rings. They also study records of ocean and surface temperatures and satellite data. This in-depth research confirms that Earth's temperature was steady for centuries before the Industrial Revolution of the 1800s. Then, Earth began to get much, much hotter.

Volcanic eruptions release carbon dioxide and other gases into the atmosphere. However, human activities produce far more emissions.

The natural greenhouse effect warms the atmosphere and Earth's surface. Without it, our planet would be too cold to support life.

Emergency Files

Greenhouse Effect

Greenhouses protect plants and keep them warm. Earth's atmosphere acts like a greenhouse, protecting our planet but allowing energy from the Sun to reach it. Earth absorbs this energy and reflects some back into space. Greenhouse gases, such as carbon dioxide and methane, trap the heat energy in Earth's atmosphere, keeping the Earth warm and livable. When levels of greenhouse gases are too high, Earth's forests, oceans, and soil cannot absorb them. The gases remain in the atmosphere, trapping energy, and heating up the planet.

Natural Causes

Many natural events affect Earth's climate, from volcanic eruptions to ocean currents. For example, El Niño and La Niña are names for climate patterns in the Pacific Ocean. Both affect climate around the world. El Niño is a pattern of usually warm surface waters that can cause flooding in South America and drought in Australia. La Niña brings cooler surface waters that can bring floods to Asia and southeast Africa but dry conditions to North and South America. El Niño may last about a year, while La Niña events may last between one and three years.

The Human Problem

In the 1800s, people started using coal to power new factories, run ships and trains, and to heat homes. Coal is still used today, especially for electric power, but oil and natural gas are commonly used in industry, transportation, and in homes. Burning these fossil fuels releases huge amounts of carbon dioxide into the atmosphere. Today, scientists estimate there is about 50 percent more carbon dioxide in the atmosphere than there was before the Industrial Revolution.

The Way We Live

The modern world relies on electricity, heat, and transportation. Yet, using non-renewable fossil fuels to produce these things is the leading cause of greenhouse gas emissions today. Carbon dioxide contributes the most to global warming, but human activities cause other greenhouse emissions. What and how we produce food has a huge impact, for example. Cows and sheep emit large amounts of methane, a powerful but shorter-lived gas. Fertilizers produce nitrous oxide. Changing how we do things is key to fighting climate change.

Motor vehicles are a major contributor to climate change. A typical car emits about 5 tons (4.6 metric tons) of carbon dioxide gas a year.

An illegal forest clearance in the Amazon rainforest in Brazil. Trees have been cut down and burned to make way for farmland.

Emergency Files

Deforestation

According to the United Nations (UN), people have cleared more than 1 billion acres (420 million hectares) of forest since 1990. This is happening even though we know that forests are essential for our planet. Forests influence water and soil and help to prevent floods. They are home to more than half of the world's land-based animals, plants, and insects. Millions of people live in forests and depend on them for food and shelter. In terms of climate change, forests are also Earth's natural "carbon sinks." Trees absorb carbon dioxide. When they are cut down or damaged, they release the carbon and other gases.

Chapter 2

Political Action

Governments around the world have a crucial role in fighting climate change. They can introduce or change laws that will help stop the causes of climate change and help to protect against further damage. By engaging with governments, climate activists can help to influence policies and force real change.

Speak Up

Youth Advisor

Jerome Foster II is a young American climate activist. When he was in high school, Jerome began protesting about climate change. He created Waic Up as online platform for young people to share news, arts, and more. In 2021, Foster became the youngest ever White House advisor when President Biden asked him to serve on the White House Environmental Justice Advisory Council.

Jerome Foster (born in 2002) went from protesting outside the White House to working with it as an advisor.

The Arc de Triomphe in Paris, France, was lit in green to celebrate the implementation of the Paris Agreement on climate change.

A total of 195 governments from around the world signed the Paris Agreement in 2015. All agreed to cut greenhouse emissions. In some countries, such as Sweden and Canada, governments introduced national carbon taxes. A carbon tax is a charge for greenhouse gas pollution. It encourages people to use cleaner processes and renewable fuels.

Net Zero

The goal of the Paris Agreement is to keep the global temperature increase below 1.5 degrees. If global warming goes beyond this, scientists warn that the effects of climate change will get much worse. To stop the temperature increase, people must find ways to cut gas emissions by 45 percent by 2030 and reach net zero emissions by 2050. Every country that signed the Paris Agreement has a climate action plan to make this happen. But these plans are not going far enough, and without immediate action, the world will not meet its targets.

Global Engagement

The United Nations (UN) held the first global climate change conference, COP, in 1995. World leaders, scientists, media, and thousands more people meet each year since. The COP is a chance for global agreement and action. In 2005, the UN introduced the Climate Change Conference for Youth (COY), now held every year. In 2022 young climate activists were invited to attend the first Children and Youth Pavilion at COP27.

Challenging Government

In 2015, Xiuhtezcatl (pronounced shoo-tez-caht) Martinez was one of 21 young people who sued the US government for failing to act on climate change. Although the lawsuit was unsuccessful, it made headlines around the world and inspired other young people to pursue their own actions against their governments.

Xiuhtezcal Martinez, also known by the initial X, has spoken out about the effects of climate change on Indigenous people around the world.

Speak Up

Green Generation

Elizabeth Wathuti, a young activist from Kenya, Africa, founded Green Generation Initiative in 2016. The organization educates and empowers children and young people to get involved in the fight against climate change. The initiative supports tree planting, including food trees, and protecting the natural environment.

Climate change has a devastating impact on the Global South. Activists from these countries, like Elizabeth, are making their voices heard.

Chapter 3

It Starts with You

Thinking about climate change can feel overwhelming. You might think that there is not much one person can do. But everyone can make a difference and become a climate activist. The ordinary choices that you make every day can have a positive impact.

Start by being a climate warrior at home. Recycle as much as you can and encourage your family to do the same. Use reusable straws and water bottles. Shop for local goods whenever possible and look for products that use little packaging.

Eat Your Vegetables

Food production, processing, and distribution has a serious impact on climate change. Make a choice to eat locally produced food as much as possible. Eat vegetables and fruit that are in season where you live. Cut down on the amount of meat you eat and consider having meat-free meals whenever you can.

Markets offer fresh, seasonal produce that is grown locally. Buying from a market also cuts down on waste and packaging.

Choosing to cycle instead of using a car reduces carbon emissions and has health benefits, too.

Your Carbon Footprint

A carbon footprint is the amount of greenhouse gases released into the air because of your daily activities. Carbon footprints are usually measured over a year and can apply to individuals, a product, organizations, or events. To keep your carbon footprint low, unplug your computer or the TV when you are not using them. Walk or ride a bike instead of taking a car ride. A car ride of just over 2 miles (3 km) puts almost 2 lb (1 kg) of carbon dioxide into the air.

Going Green

There are many ways to change the way you live every day. Some of these changes are simple, such as not using a plastic straw. Sometimes, it might be difficult. Traveling on a plane, for example, might be the only way you can reach a destination. Day by day, it is up to you to make the best choices available to help to fight climate change.

Trees absorb harmful greenhouse gases. Planting trees, and tending existing ones, can help combat climate change.

Planting Trees

Tree planting is something anyone can do in their communities. It is one of the ways young people are helping fight climate change all over the world. In Uganda, Africa, two university students started My Tree Initiative. They work with local councils to organize tree planting days for schools. Groups like this are springing up all over the world. Find a local tree planting group or start one of your own.

The fashion industry accounts for one tenth of the greenhouse gas emissions produced by human activity. Upcycling clothes is an easy and creative way to tackle this problem.

Reusing, Recycling, and Upcycling

A lot of our garbage ends up in landfills and is burned, sending more pollutants into the atmosphere. By reusing and recycling what we can, we save energy and reduce greenhouse gases. Upcycling is taking an old product, such as furniture or an item of clothing, and giving it a new look or purpose. Before you throw something away, consider if there is something else you can do with it.

Chapter 4

Stand Together

Many people believe that governments and other organizations are too slow to act. They put pressure on them to act more quickly. They do this through protest and direct action.

A growing movement of activists believes that only direct political action will bring about the change that is needed. Different groups are staging protests to raise public awareness and to try to force governments to take action.

Tactics

The groups use different tactics. Extinction Rebellion (XR), founded in 2018, causes widespread disruption in cities. XR activists use tactics known as civil disobedience, which were used by civil rights campaigners in the 1960s. They refuse to obey the law, but they do not use violence. In Paris, France, Parkour activists use their free-running skills to turn off store lights that are being left on all night.

Extinction Rebellion supporters take part in a "die-in" protest. The group uses non-violent peaceful actions to highlight its demands.

Greta Thunberg (center). Fridays for the Future combines large demonstrations with advocacy and on-line protest.

Speak Up

Fridays for the Future

Swedish schoolgirl Greta Thunberg was only 15 years old in August 2018, when she began to take every Friday off school to protest climate change outside the Swedish parliament. Initially alone, she was soon joined by other students. They created the hashtag #FridaysForFuture and encouraged other students to join them. The idea spread to other countries and now involves millions of people who organize local protests for international demands. The youth-led movement, Fridays for the Future, calls for immediate action on climate change, including keeping global temperature increases below 1.5 degrees.

Choosing a Cause

Some climate activists focus on specific causes or changes. These specific campaigns make a major contribution to the overall fight against climate change. Youth-led movements have forced institutions and governments to act.

Fossil Fuel

Beginning in the United States in 2011, university students began a campaign to force their school to divest from fossil fuels. This means to stop their schools from investing in or making money from fossil fuels. The Fossil Free movement spread to the United Kingdom and around the world. Since it began, the movement has forced over 1,590 institutions to divest $40 trillion.

Youth activists call for an end to the use of fossil fuels and for investment in renewable forms of energy instead.

Farmers use about 26 percent of the world's land for grazing. And livestock emit methane, which is a greenhouse gas.

Speak Up

Plant-Based Eating

Animal agriculture is a leading cause of methane gas emissions. When she was just 10 years old, Genesis Butler gave a Tedx talk, "A 10 Year Old's Vision for Healing the Planet." The inspiring talk explained the harmful effects of animal agriculture. As she grew older, Genesis realized that many other young people were passionate about this issue. She founded Youth Climate Save, the first youth climate movement to focus on the connection between animal agriculture and climate change. She also used her voice to force a change in California law. The law now requires hospitals, prisons, and nursing homes to offer vegan meal options.

Indigenous Voices

Indigenous people around the world have been caretakers of Earth for thousands of years. Their cultures and many of their traditions are entwined with preserving the balance of nature. Today, young Indigenous activists are leading the struggle against climate change.

Saving the Rainforest

Artemisa Xakriabá is a member of the Xakriaba tribe in southeastern Brazil who live in the Amazon rainforest. The tribe depends on the natural resources of the rainforest, including water from the river. But Earth also relies on the rainforest as a massive carbon sink. As forest fires, mining, and farming destroy the Amazon, carbon emissions are soaring.

Nearly 20 percent of the Amazon rainforest has been cut down in the last 50 years. Following his election in 2022, Brazilian President Lula da Silva promised to end deforestation by 2030.

Ta'kaiya Blaney believes that young activists have the power to create change, by speaking out and taking action.

Speak Up

Fighting Big Oil

Ta'kaiya Blaney was 10 years old when she released a song, "Shallow Waters," warning of the effects of oil spills. As an actor and singer, Ta'kaiya, a member of the Tla'Amin First Nation in British Columbia, Canada, uses her art to raise awareness about climate issues and Indigenous rights. She has spoken and performed at rallies, forums, and conferences across the world, including the UN Climate Change Conference in 2021.

Pacific Warriors

350 Pacific is a grassroots youth movement. It brings together 18 island nations in the Pacific Ocean as well as communities in Australia, New Zealand, and the United States. Pacific islands are particularly vulnerable to the impacts of climate change with rising sea levels and severe storms. In addition, heatwaves and ocean acidification threaten health and livelihoods.

Chapter 5

Your Activist Toolkit

There are many ways to get involved in the climate change fight. Join the millions of young people already working to save the planet. The important thing is to start.

You can begin by finding out what climate action groups exist in your community. If there is nothing nearby, you can join groups online and consider starting your own group.

Setting Goals

Think about what you want to achieve. Maybe you want to get involved in greening your community. Perhaps you want more people to try going vegan. Could you help your school use less paper? What other changes would you like to see where you live? Make a list. Think about setting some smaller goals first and build on those to achieve larger ones.

A lot of information is available online. Use the internet to find existing campaign groups and to spread your message.

Placards are a great way to make a statement. Making placards can be fun. Get together with other activists and make it a group activity.

Getting Prepared

Once you know what you want to do and how you want to get involved, you need to prepare. Educate yourself on the issue and have the facts to back you up. Look for courses you can take or seminars you can attend. Read up on the latest science. Sign up for free newsletters from established climate action organizations. Find out how other young people have started their campaigns. Think about the skills you have, such as being great at making connections with people or being good at art and design. How could these skills be used? Some organizations even offer training programs for youth climate activism. Many of these are online. Check them out.

Taking Action

You have identified your goals and done your research. Now you are ready to make things happen. Many organizations need volunteers. You can help in person, if it is a local group, or see what you can do virtually. Groups usually need help with fundraising, preparing for events, distributing information, and much more.

Organize an Event

People like to participate in events for a cause. You can arrange an event that raises awareness and money for climate change. Hold a movie night at your school featuring a film about climate change. Create a community garden or organize a fun run or cycling event. Make sure that you find out about local bylaws and permits before you hold an event.

Community gardens provide food and build a connection between people and the environment.

Climate change affects the lives of young people everywhere. You're never too young to join a protest!

Protests

Gatherings and marches bring people together and send a powerful message. See what events are already happening around you. Tell everyone you know and encourage them to attend. Make a sign and participate.

Social Media

Using online social networks is an amazing way to reach many people and get your message out there. It has the potential to reach people everywhere. You can deliver information, share news, promote events, and spread awareness. Most well-known climate activists and organizations already have a social media presence. Follow and support them and forward the messages wherever you can.

Timeline

1970	The first Earth Day (April 22 each year) about 20 million people across the United States rallied in protest
1972	Stockholm Conference
1987	Montreal Protocol restricts the use of chemicals that damage the ozone
1992	First Earth Summit in Rio de Janeiro, Brazil
1995	First UN Climate Change Conference in Berlin, Germany
2001	Campaign Against Climate Change founded in the United Kingdom
February 2005	Kyoto Protocol assigns maximum carbon emission levels for countries
November 2005	Conference of Youth (COY) formed
December 2005	First Global Day of Action on Climate Change
2011	Official Youth Constituency of the UNFCCC (YouNGO) becomes official; it brings together youth organizations and individuals working with the United Nations Framework Convention on Climate Change (UNFCCC)
2014	People's Climate March, New York City
2016	Paris Agreement comes into effect, replacing the Kyoto Protocol
August 2018	Greta Thunberg holds the first school strike

October 2018	Extinction Rebellion stages its first non-violent protest action
March 2019	First global School Strike for Climate
September 2019	UN holds the Climate Youth Summit in New York
September 2019	Global Week for Future; millions strike in protest across the world
2020	UN launches Youth Advisory Group on Climate Change
2021	European Climate Law sets a goal to reach climate neutrality by 2050
2022	First Children and Youth Pavilion at COP27
2023	Global Greenhouse Gas Watch approved to monitor emissions

Youth vs Apocalypse is a youth-led climate justice group. As well as organizing protests, it helps students set up climate action clubs in schools.

Glossary

acidification in oceans, change in the chemical balance of seawater due to too much carbon dioxide leading to harmful effects on sea animals and plants

activist A person working to create change for the better

atmosphere layers of gases that surround and protect Earth

climate change the change in Earth's climate over a long period of time

deforestation removing forest from land to use the land for another purpose

drought an extended period of time without enough rain

emissions substances, such as gases, sent out into the air

fertilizer chemical or natural substance added to soil or plants to improve plant growth

fossil fuel fuel such as coal and oil that form from animals and plants that died long ago

fundraising collecting money for a cause or charity

Global South countries with a relatively low level of economic and industrial development

global warming gradual increase in Earth's overall temperature

grassroots describes movements or groups of people who are not in positions of power

greenhouse gas gas such as carbon dioxide, methane, and nitrous oxide that trap heat

habitat natural home of an animal or plant

Indigenous native to a specific place

Industrial Revolution period that saw the change from making goods by hand to using machines

net zero a state in which levels of greenhouse gases going into the atmosphere are balanced by the removal out of the atmosphere

non-renewable not able to made again

Further Information

Books

Gehl, Laura. *Climate Warriors: Fourteen Scientists and Fourteen Ways We Can Save Our Planet.* Millbrook Press, 2023

Hooke, Dan. *Climate Emergency Atlas.* DK Children, 2020

Klein, Naomi. Stefoff, Rebecca (Adapter). *How to Change Everything.* Atheneum Books, 2021

Meek, Amy and Ella. *Be Climate Clever.* DK Children, 2022

Sjonger, Rebecca. *Taking Action to Help the Environment (UN Sustainable Development Goals).* Crabtree Publishing, 2020

Thunberg, Greta. *No One is Too Small to Make a Difference.* Penguin Books, 2019

Websites

fridaysforfuture.org
Information on the Fridays for Future movement, its actions, and how to get involved.

gofossilfree.org
Includes information about how the world can go fossil free as well as training and advice for individual and group action.

kidsagainstclimatechange.co
Site sponsored by the US Ocean Service (NOAA) with several links to books, videos, and websites for further information.

www.thisiszerohour.org
Youth led movement started in 2017 includes access to Zero Hour 101, a virtual training program for young activists.

Index